PET OWNER'S GUIDE TO
TROPICAL
FISHKEEPING

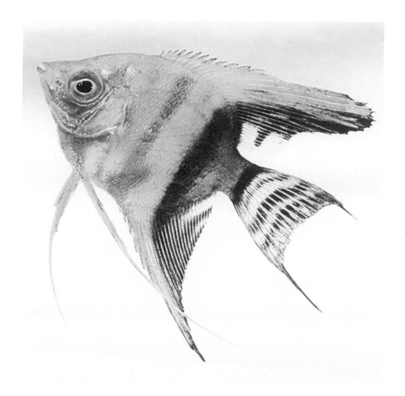

Mary Bailey

RINGPRESS

ABOUT THE AUTHOR

Mary Bailey has been keeping tropical fishes for more than 25 years, and is known internationally as an expert on the cichlid family. She writes regularly for fishkeeping magazines in the UK and overseas, as well as being a contributor to and co-editor of the Cichlids Yearbook series and English editor of *aqua geographia* magazine. She has one earlier book on fishkeeping to her credit: *The Ultimate Aquarium*, co-written by Gina Sandford. She lives in the wilds of the Devon countryside with her fishes, cats, and horse.

ACKNOWLEDGEMENTS

The author would like to thank Gina Sandford and Nick Fletcher for critically reading the manuscript.

Published by Ringpress Books Limited,
PO Box 8, Lydney, Gloucestershire,
GL15 6YD, United Kingdom.

First published 1998
©1998 Ringpress Books Limited. All rights reserved

ISBN 1 86054 067 8

Printed in Hong Kong through Printworks Int. Ltd.

CONTENTS

1 Introduction to Tropical Fishkeeping

People have been keeping ornamental coldwater fishes for millennia, but it is only recently that maintaining their tropical cousins in captivity has become widespread in temperate zones, with the advent of the electrical equipment necessary to make the hobby practicable.

Generally speaking, the term "tropical fishes" encompasses species found naturally only in water with an annual minimum temperature of 65 degrees

Fahrenheit (18.5 Celsius) or higher, that is at relatively low altitudes between the Tropics of Cancer and Capricorn. Bodies of water in mountainous regions in this zone, for example on the *alto plano* of Peru, are more akin in temperature to the lakes and rivers of temperate regions. In practice, however, the group also includes a number of species from relatively warm waters north and south of these arbitrary dividing lines, for example in Florida and the Middle East. Because of its climate the former is, in fact, a major centre for the commercial breeding of "tropicals", many of which have escaped and established feral populations in the region.

DIFFERENT SPECIES

Many thousands of different species of fishes are found in tropical freshwaters, and the number kept in captivity easily runs to four figures. It has to be said that not all are really suited to aquarium culture, sometimes because of their eventual large size, sometimes because of their behaviour, and sometimes because of their specialised requirements – nevertheless there is usually an aquarist somewhere who will try, despite the problems. As a

beginner, you will do best to gain some experience with easy-to-maintain and readily available species, before considering moving on to something more challenging if that is your inclination. On the other hand, you may simply want to create a living underwater scene to ornament your home.

RESPONSIBILITIES

When considering keeping fishes in indoor aquaria, it is essential to be aware of their total dependence on their owner; their entire environment is under his or her management. Unlike dogs and cats and many other domestic animals, fishes do not have the option of fending for themselves if neglected by their owner, and will not live long without the necessary attention. But provided you are prepared to accept this responsibility – which will require only an hour or two in total each week – fishkeeping can be a most enjoyable and rewarding hobby.

HELPING HANDS

Fishkeeping in isolation is fun, fishkeeping with friends even more so – with the added advantage that when something goes wrong (as it inevitably will, sooner or later), then there are people you can call upon to help. Fishkeeping friends can be a source of advice and physical assistance (it takes two to carry all but the smallest aquarium), of fishes and spare equipment, and they can also act as holiday fish-minders. You must, of course, repay them in kind whenever you are able.

The best way of meeting other fishkeepers is to join your local club; most clubs meet once a month, with activities including shows, discussions, talks and slide shows, and auctions of fishes, plants, and equipment. It is not always easy to contact your local club, but you should be able to find out the necessary information from a local aquatic dealer.

CHOOSING A DEALER

One of the best fishkeeping friends you can make is a good dealer, with the emphasis on the 'good' as there are many whose main interest is money in the till rather than giving free advice. To 'try out' a

dealer, pick a quiet time when the shop is quiet (e.g. first thing on a weekday morning). Talk to the dealer, or the member of staff with specialist fish knowledge, and outline your plans for setting up an aquarium. If you are given advice and information which concurs with the general principles outlined in this book, you will know you are on the right lines. However, if there is an attempt to sell you tank, equipment and fish there and then – or a marked lack of interest – take your custom elsewhere!

Of course, you may want to shop elsewhere from time to time, but if you find a really good dealer, it is worth maintaining mutual goodwill by patronising the shop whenever possible. You may well need extra advice as you pursue your fishkeeping career.

THE PURSUIT OF KNOWLEDGE

You will never learn all there is to learn about fishkeeping and fishes – aquarists with thirty or more years experience behind them will freely admit they are still learning. This is part of the fun! No matter if a new piece of knowledge appears useless at the time – one day it may come in handy. For this reason, I would urge you to make an active effort to learn – talk to other aquarists, go to talks and slideshows, and, above all, read everything you can lay hands on. You may find differing opinions on some topics, but if you follow the consensus you should not go far wrong.

2 *Planning Your Aquarium*

Creating a successful aquarium is not simply a matter of filling a glass box with water and adding fishes – it is a complex project that requires careful planning, otherwise a number of disasters lie in wait for the unwary. You have a lot of learning to do, and it is best if you grasp the basics before you start, rather than learning by your mistakes as you go along.

An astonishing number of would-be aquarists who buy and set up an aquarium and only then decide what to put in it and suffer immense frustration when they discover it is too small, or otherwise unsuitable, for the fishes they would prefer. Or worse, they go ahead regardless, and end up with an aquatic battlefield or graveyard. You must consider all the variables involved in advance – aquarium size and position, choice of fishes, etc. Never compromise the fishes' welfare in order to satisfy your preferences. Remember, it is their home that you are creating, their lives that are in your hands, their needs that must come first.

WHAT SIZE AQUARIUM?

The size of your aquarium will depend on factors such as how much you can afford, where you

Hexagonal tank.

height of the aquarium will be limited by its position, remember that you will need at least 5 ins (12.5 cms) to accommodate the baseboard and hood (see Chapter Four: Equipment) and for access, in addition to the depth of the tank itself.

A common mistake is to buy a very small aquarium on the basis that this is your first experimental venture into fishkeeping. Small aquaria are more difficult to keep healthy, and lead to almost instant frustration because you can put very few fishes in them. The quantity of fishes an aquarium can accommodate is usually calculated in terms of their average oxygen requirement, and expressed as inches or centimetres of fish (not including the tail) relative to aquarium surface area (its length x its width). As a general guideline, you should allow 10 square inches (64 sq cms) of surface area per inch (2.5cms) of fish, though behavioural factors (e.g. the need of some species to hold territory) may indicate a lower population density. Always use the eventual, full-grown size of the fishes in your calculations.

A large aquarium is more versatile in the event that your preferences change later on: you

A rectangular tank and cabinet.

are going to put it, and what you propose to put in it. As well as the length and breadth you must consider the depth: some fishes have deep bodies and/or long trailing finnage, and require deeper aquaria than the most usual 15 ins (approx 40cms). Then again, if you plan to keep only small bottom-dwellers such as dwarf species of cichlids and catfishes, 8 or 10 ins (20 or 25cms) may be adequate. If the

A corner tank.

can keep a 4 inch (10 cms) fish in a 48 inch (120 cms) aquarium, but not a 12 inch (30 cms) one in an 18 inch (45 cms) tank! If you have the space and money, start with at least a 36 inch (90 cms) tank, better a 48 inch, which will give you reasonable scope.

WHERE TO PUT IT

The aquarium should be sited where it will not be liable to chance knocks from passers-by or carelessly moved furniture, but equally, if it is to be enjoyed to the full, it should be clearly visible, not stuck in a dark corner.

Constant passing traffic (especially boisterous children and pets) may lead to nervous fishes, but so may a secluded position which gives the occupants no chance to get used to people. The living-room is the obvious choice, so that the family can enjoy the aquarium during their leisure time; then again, spillages are inevitable, so, if you have an expensive new carpet, a different room may be preferable. Remember that, once filled, an aquarium is too heavy to move if you change your mind! Relocating it will mean starting almost from scratch.

The weight of the aquarium must also be considered when selecting the site. A gallon of water weighs 10lbs (4.55 kg), so a 50-gallon (228 litre) aquarium will weigh about quarter of a ton in total. If you plan to use a built-in feature as your base, it must be strong enough to bear the load, as must your floor if you are using a cabinet or stand. Always site a large (more than 36 ins/90cms) aquarium against a wall and with its long dimension across (at right-angles to) the joists, to spread the load. If in any doubt, seek professional advice.

The aquarium should also be within sensible distance of an

electric point, and, if possible, a water supply. Carting water between a ground floor supply and loft conversion aquarium will keep you fit, but... You will also want easy access for routine maintenance, without having to move the furniture every time you feed the fishes.

CHOICE OF FISHES

A huge variety of fishes is available, and, like every other beginner faced with this choice, you will undoubtedly want to keep most of them. This is, obviously, impossible; less obvious is the fact that, even if you compile a shortlist of those you fancy, they may not all be suitable for your aquarium. They may be incompatible with one another in a number of ways: some fishes are highly territorial and will attack their tankmates, some will eat them, some have different requirements as regards water conditions (see Chapter Three) and surroundings (Chapter Five). It is no use mixing such incompatible fishes – it will not be successful in the long term, and may lead to discomfort or death for them, and disappointment for you.

If your ambition is to create an attractive underwater garden, then beware of species that eat plants, or convert the aquarium into a moonscape with their digging. Some may have difficult or distasteful dietary requirements; not everyone enjoys feeding one fish to another, but there are species which will eat only live fish. You cannot change their habits because you disapprove, and you should not try.

There are, however, plenty of fishes that will live harmoniously together if you want a mixed community aquarium. Or, if you prefer, you can keep one of the "trouble causers" – by itself! The important thing is to find out (read or ask) about the habits and requirements of any fish before buying it – not afterwards. And if in doubt, do not buy it.

THE MAIN GROUPS OF TROPICAL FRESHWATER FISHES

The following is a brief overview of the fishes you are likely to encounter. It is not intended to be a comprehensive guide, and, as already stressed, it is essential to find out about each individual species before purchase, to make sure it is suitable for your aquarium and vice versa.

ANABANTIDS OR LABYRINTH FISHES

Often also referred to as "bubblenest builders". A large group of tropical fishes found in Africa and Asia, best known for their ability to breathe atmospheric air using a

Paradise fish *(Macropodus opercularis)*.

Dwarf gourami *(Colisa lalia)*.

special organ called the labyrinth – their natural waters are often poor in dissolved oxygen. They normally swim in the middle and upper layers of the aquarium. The group includes gouramies, fighting fishes, combtails, and paradise fishes, and some are good community fishes.

Siamese fighting fish – female *(Betta splendens)*.

Size range: 1 to 30 ins (2.5 to 75 cms) or more.
Diet: Many are insectivorous; most can be maintained on dried foods, but all

benefit from live or frozen foods, especially as a preliminary to breeding.

Breeding: Some species build nests of bubbles at the surface (where oxygen content is highest), some produce floating eggs, and some guard their eggs in their mouths. Parental care is generally by the male.

Problem areas: Must have an air space between the water's surface and any cover

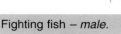

Fighting fish – *male*.

glass/condensation tray, as they will "drown" without access to atmospheric air. Their long ventral

Opaline gourami *(Trichogaster trichopterus)*.

fins are prone to nipping by other fishes; some species can become quite aggressive, and male fighting fishes will fight to the death if kept together. Paternal males may attack females, who should be removed after spawning.

CATFISHES

An extremely diverse group of fishes occurring pan-globally in salt as well as fresh water, but found primarily in tropical freshwaters (of varying chemistry). All catfishes have barbels, the "whiskers" that have given them their common name, which are highly sensitive taste organs used to locate food. Unlike

Plecostomus catfish *(Hypostomus sp.)*.

most fishes they do not have scales, but instead are protected by thick skin or bony plates called scutes. Most are bottom dwellers, and many are nocturnal.

Bristlenose catfish *(Ancistus sp.)*.

Whiptail catfish *(Rineloricaria sp.)*.

Size range: 1 inch to 8 feet (2.5 cms to 2.5 m) or more.

Diet: Highly variable, depending on species; the group includes herbivores and some formidable predators. Although they are often regarded as scavengers which will make do with any food left by the other fishes, proper nourishment with a correct diet is essential.

Breeding: Egg-layers. Some species practise parental care of eggs and fry. At least one species is a "cuckoo", which substitutes its eggs for those of mouthbrooding cichlids while they are spawning. Breeding is generally regarded as difficult.

Problem areas: A fine substrate is advisable for bottom-dwellers to prevent damage to delicate barbels. The stout, sharp pectoral and dorsal spines may cause nasty injuries if mishandled, and can easily become entangled in the net, so handle with care.

Silver hatchet (*Gasteropelecus sternicla*).

CHARACINS

A large group of fishes from South and Central America and Africa, many of them shoaling species. The group includes tetras, pencilfishes, hatchetfishes,

Head and tail light tetra, also known as the beaconfish.

headstanders – and piranhas. Many are small and colourful, and excellent fishes for the general community. Others are quite unsuitable: they may grow very

X-ray tetra (*Pristella riddlei*).

large, and/or be predatory, aggressive, or inimical to plants – so always check! Most come from soft, acid water, but many have been acclimated to harder, more

Penguin tetra (*Thayeria boehlkei*), also known as the penguinfish.

alkaline conditions; almost all require excellent water quality. Most, especially smaller species,

Neon Tetra (*Paracheirodon innesi*).

require the security of a shoal (6 or more) of their own kind, or they may hide and not feed. Active fishes which require plenty of swimming space in the middle and upper layers of the aquarium.

Size range: $^3/_4$ to 40 ins (2 to 100 cms) or more.

Diet: Varies according to species; most of the smaller species are insectivores which will do well on flake and granules, but benefit from live and frozen foods.

Breeding: Correct water conditions essential. Most spawn among plants and do not subsequently tend their eggs, but some of the larger species practise brood care.

Problem areas: Small characins commonly fall prey to larger (or large-mouthed) tankmates, even if the latter are not particularly piscivorous. Hatchetfishes are sensitive to incorrect water conditions, and jump, so a tight-fitting cover is needed. Piranhas are dangerous to other fishes and their owner; the aquarium must be child-proof. Herbivores such as silver dollars (*Metynnis argenteus*) will strip an aquarium of vegetation. *Phago* eats the fins of other fishes.

Pseudotropheus zebra (Lake Malawi).

CICHLIDS

An extremely diverse family of perch-like fishes, found only in the tropics, and restricted largely to

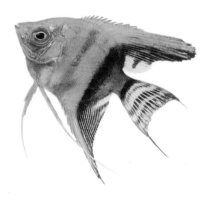

Half black angel (*Pterophyllum scalare*).

Africa and the Americas, with a few representatives in the Middle East and the Indian sub-continent. Many are highly coloured, but their main attraction for aquarists is their apparent intelligence, undoubted character, and devoted

Koi angel (*Pterophyllum scalare*).

brood care. Unfortunately the latter makes many unsuitable for the community aquarium, as they are generally fiercely territorial in the defence of their brood. Most are rather bottom-orientated and require some sort of hiding-place.

Size range: ³/4 in to 36 ins (2 to 90 cms).

Diet: Highly variable, depending on species. The family includes herbivores and piscivores, and some remarkable feeding adaptations such as scale-eaters, egg-robbers, and cleaner-fishes.

Breeding: Two main strategies: substrate brooding, where the eggs are laid on a stone, plant, or other substrate and guarded by one or both parents; and mouthbrooding, where the eggs are taken into the mouth of one or both parents for protection.

Problem areas: Some species can be extremely hostile to tankmates, even when not actively breeding; considerable care is required in selecting species for a community

Giant danio *(Danio aequipinnatus)*.

setting. Most species dig as a preliminary to breeding, to create nursery pits or prepare a spawning site. Many species are prone to digestive troubles if fed an unsuitable diet.

CYPRINIDS

This large group is native to Africa, Europe, Asia, and southern North America, and, as well as

Sucking loach *(Gyrinocheilus)*, also known as the Chinese algae eater.

tropical species, includes such well-known coldwater fishes as the goldfish and carp. The tropical group includes such popular aquarium fishes as barbs, rasboras, danios, "sharks", and loaches. Not all are suitable for the community aquarium, in size and/or habits. Most are best kept in small groups or shoals. The group includes

Tiger barb *(Barbus tetrazona)*.

bottom-orientated (loaches) and mid-water species.

Size range: $^3/_4$ in to 24 ins (2 to 60 cms) or more.

Diet: Varies from species to species; the smaller species tend to be omnivorous or insectivorous, while some large species are herbivores.

Breeding: Egg-layers (often on or among plants) which do not practise parental care.

Problem areas: "Sharks" and some loaches can be territorial and harass tankmates; some small

Gold Mickey Mouse platy *(Xiphophorus sp.).*

barbs are notorious fin-nippers, though this is less likely if they are kept in a shoal.

CYPRINODONTS (TOOTHCARPS)
Cyprinodonts are found in the

Green sailfin molly *(Poecillia sp.).*

tropical Americas, Africa, and Asia, and one or two species come from somewhat cooler waters. Their natural waters range from very soft and acid to hard and alkaline or even brackish.

This group of small, usually surface-living and insectivorous, fishes is subdivided into two sections: the livebearing toothcarps, which include some of the hardiest and most popular aquarium fishes such as guppies, platies, swordtails, and mollies; and the egg-laying toothcarps or

Red swordtail *(Xiphophorus sp.).*

Orange marbled molly *(Poecillia sp.).*

Silver shark (*Balantiocheilus melanopterus*).

killifishes, most of which are regarded as subjects for the specialist. Some "killies" are annual fishes, which come from temporary pools and have a natural lifespan of less than a year. They lay eggs before their pool dries up, and these hatch into a new generation when the rains come.

Red tailed black shark (*Epalzeorhynchus bicolor*).

Fancy strains of many of the livebearing toothcarps have been developed from the original wild forms, while some of the killifishes are among the most colourful of tropical fishes. The livebearing species are often known simply as "livebearers", but there are in fact also non-cyprinodonts which produce live young and thus come under that generalised heading.

Size range: $3/4$ in to 9.5 ins (2 to 24 cms).

Diet: Most livebearing toothcarps will thrive on dried foods, though live and frozen foods are appreciated. Some are partially herbivorous. Killifishes, by contrast, require live or frozen foods, though may take some flake.

Breeding: Neither group practises brood care. As their name implies, livebearers are fertilised internally and give birth to fry; killifishes are egg-layers, the annual species spawning in the bottom mud (peat is used in the aquarium), the others on plants or special spawning mops. The eggs of those from annual pools have to be dried out, stored, and returned to water after an appropriate period, to simulate the natural process.

Problem areas: Livebearers commonly eat their fry unless preventive measures (e.g. breeding traps) are taken. Killifishes are "fiddly" (but great fun) and best kept in single-species aquaria.

Annual killies are very short-lived, and all are accomplished jumpers, so a tight-fitting hood is essential.

MISCELLANEOUS SMALL GROUPS

BICHIRS AND REEDFISHES

Elongated, rather snake-like, African fishes with a swimbladder modified to enable them to breathe atmospheric air, and which suffocate if prevented from doing so. They are predators which will eat smaller tankmates, and require a tight-fitting hood or they will wriggle out of the aquarium.

Asian glass catfish (Kryptopterus bicirrhis).

ELECTRIC FISHES

A number of fishes from quite different families are able to generate an electrical charge, sometimes weak (used for navigational purposes), and sometimes powerful (for defence or to stun prey). The former include elephant noses and knifefishes; the latter electric eels, which are dangerous and unsuitable for beginners. All are specialist fishes.

GLASSFISHES

Rather delicate transparent fishes which benefit from their own aquarium. Live and frozen foods preferred. Avoid specimens which have been injected with fluorescent dye to make them "more attractive" – they are unlikely to live long.

GOBIES

Carnivorous bottom-dwellers, sometimes territorial, which require hiding-places such as caves. Many are brackish-water fishes, but some species come from fresh water. Some are suitable for the community aquarium.

HALFBEAKS

Shoaling, surface-dwelling, live-bearing insectivores (live food required in captivity) from south-east Asia. The elongated lower jaw (the "half-beak") is easily damaged; handle with care, and avoid buying damaged specimens, which are unlikely to live long.

LEAF FISHES

Members of a number of genera

from South America, Africa, and Asia, with the common feature of a leaf-like appearance. This camouflage allows them to ambush prey, which will include small community fishes! Some will eat only live fish.

Celebes rainbow fish *(Telmatherina ladigesi)*.

SNAKEHEADS
Large (6-36 ins/ 15-90 cms) predatory fishes which make excellent pets but are unsuitable for the general community.

SPINY EELS
Eel-like burrowing fishes from Africa and south-east Asia. Live or frozen foods preferred, and they may prey on small tankmates. Can attain 30 ins (75 cms).

RAINBOWFISHES
Small (most smaller than 6 ins/15 cms), generally peaceful, colourful, shoaling fishes from Africa and Australasia. Most are suitable for the community if water conditions are appropriate and there is plenty of open swimming space – they are very active swimmers.

Australian rainbow fish *(Melanotaenia splendida)*.

3 *The Aquatic Environment*

Fishes inhabit a totally different medium – water – to ourselves, and if we do not provide (and maintain) that water in the condition they require, it may be tantamount to asking air-breathers to live in a room thick with smoke or poisonous gases. Thus a basic understanding of the chemistry of water, and of the biological processes that take place in this, to us, alien environment, is essential for long-term success.

WATER CHEMISTRY

Water – both that from our domestic taps and that found in natural lakes, pools, and rivers – may be hard or soft, acid, neutral, or alkaline, depending on the quantity and type of minerals dissolved in it. The measurement of these minerals is termed its hardness, and that of the acidity/alkalinity its pH, and together these constitute the basic water chemistry. Test equipment is available to enable aquarists to check hardness and pH.

Fishes are found in waters of varying chemistry, and their systems are adapted to the water of their natural home. Some are "hardy", and will live happily in almost any water, but others are far more sensitive, and may become ill, or die, if the conditions are incorrect. It is thus vital to make sure that the aquarium water is suited to its occupants – even hardy species benefit from being provided with the conditions they would enjoy in nature. Generally speaking, hard water species are more tolerant of soft water than vice versa, while both groups may react badly to incorrect pH.

Because the biochemistry of a fish interacts on multiple levels with the water in which it lives, sudden large changes in water chemistry must be avoided or death from chemical shock is likely. Bear this in mind when buying new fishes or changing part of the aquarium water. If necessary, fill the quarantine aquarium with water whose chemistry matches that to which your new fishes are accustomed, then adjust this gradually over several weeks to that of your main aquarium; likewise adjust the chemistry of water used for partial changes, before use.

Altering the chemistry of tap water is sometimes difficult, so you may find it preferable to keep fishes suited to what you can easily provide. Do not expect sensitive fishes to adapt, as they will generally take the "or die" option; putting a soft, acid water fish into hard alkaline water is just as likely to be fatal as putting a marine fish into fresh water or a tropical one into an unheated aquarium.

HARDNESS

Hardness is generally measured in terms of calcium carbonate content, in degrees, with 0-4 considered soft, 5-10 slightly to moderately hard, and 11+ very hard. In nature, water acquires hardness by dissolving soluble minerals from the terrain over which it flows, and water for the aquarium can be made harder using the same principle: calciferous material (limestone, coral, crushed shell) can form part of the decor or filter media (see below).

Unfortunately making hard water soft is not so easy. There are two main methods: firstly, it can be "diluted" using uncontaminated rain water, distilled water, or water which has been passed through a reverse osmosis (RO) unit, which, like distillation, removes everything except the basic H_2O molecule. This includes free oxygen, so distilled and RO water must always be re-oxygenated (by aeration) before use, or the fishes will suffocate.

Alternatively, water can be softened using ion-exchange resins (use only those designed for aquarium use), which do not actually reduce the mineral content, but instead alter the type of mineral salts. The water tests soft, but its total mineral content is still high – and our "soft water" fishes generally come from mineral-depleted waters. So ion-exchange is not the ideal option.

If only a small reduction in hardness is required, boiling the water will remove some of the dissolved salts.

pH

pH is measured on a scale running from 0-14, with 0 very acid, 14 very alkaline, and 7 neutral. Most fishes come from waters in the range 5.5 to 9.0. The scale is logarithmic, that is, each stage up or down from neutral is 10 times the previous one, so pH 10 is 10 times more alkaline than pH 9, and 100 times more than pH 8, and apparently small variations may in fact have a serious effect on the aquarium occupants.

The pH of water, like its hardness, is a function of substances dissolved in it;

pH test kit.

alkalinity results from dissolved minerals, and acidity from dissolved carbon dioxide and organic material. Acid water is normally soft as well, because the presence of the minerals that cause hardness normally buffers the pH to neutral or alkaline. It is thus pointless trying to acidify your water in the presence of such minerals.

Although it is possible to buy chemical agents for altering pH, it is far safer to use natural agents – calciferous materials such as limestone chips, coral sand, or crushed shell to increase pH, peat to reduce it (peat soon becomes "spent" and needs to be renewed regularly). The organic processes that take place in the aquarium tend to have a gradual acidifying effect, so, if keeping fishes which require an alkaline pH, it is wise to include some calciferous material in the system to buffer the pH to the correct level.

WATER QUALITY

The quality of aquarium water is a measure of its content of substances which are, or may be, inimical to the well-being of the occupants; that is, pollutants. These may be inorganic (chemicals) or organic, that is, by-

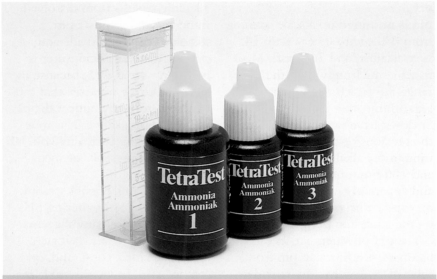

Ammonia test kit.

products of the life process. Creating and maintaining good water quality is the aquarist's most important task, and a continuing process for as long as the aquarium is maintained.

INORGANIC CONTAMINANTS

Although there are strict legal requirements for the quality of tap water in the UK, what is deemed to be safe for humans may be lethal to small fishes. Tap water may contain metallic salts accumulated from a natural source or from the domestic pipework, lead and copper being two major offenders. In addition, water companies routinely add chemicals such as chlorine and chloramine to sterilise the water, and may periodically flush the mains with insecticide to eliminate any creepy-crawlies living there. All these chemicals are toxic to fishes. Your water company will normally, on request, supply an analysis of your tap water, and although under no obligation to do so, may agree to warn you when it intends to use insecticide.

Water conditioners are available to make safe water containing copper, chlorine, and chloramine. If your water company uses only chlorine, then this can be eliminated by leaving the water to stand overnight, and the process can be speeded up by aeration. Unless your water reeks of chlorine, simply running the tap hard into a bucket normally does the trick. To avoid metallic contamination from your pipework, run the tap for a few minutes before drawing water for the aquarium in order to get rid of water that has been standing in the pipes. Never use water from the (copper) hot water cylinder.

Inorganic contamination can also occur in the aquarium from items of equipment not intended for aquarium use, and from inappropriate decor items. Avoid metal objects, use only food grade plastic items (including buckets and water storage containers), and choose your decor with care (see Chapter Five: Aquarium Decor).

ORGANIC POLLUTION AND THE NITROGEN CYCLE

All living things produce organic waste, and when they die they become wastes! Obviously the world would become a rather unpleasant place if all this rubbish accumulated continuously, but in practice it is broken down during

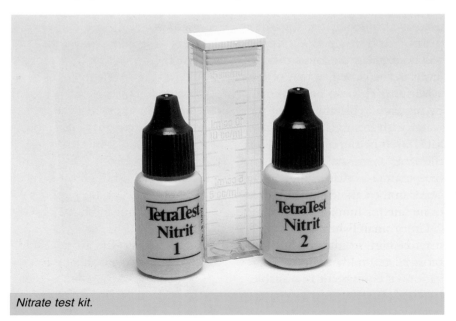

Nitrate test kit.

the process known as the nitrogen cycle, in which bacteria convert the wastes to organic chemicals which can be re-utilised by higher life forms. The nitrogen cycle takes place anywhere there is life, including the aquarium.

The first stage in the cycle is the production of ammonia (also excreted "neat" by fishes), followed by nitrite, and finally nitrate. The first two are highly toxic, but if the cycle is functioning properly then conversion to nitrate is so quick that no significant build-up of toxins occurs. Nitrate is relatively harmless, and some of it will be used as fertiliser by the aquarium plants, but over a period of time it will accumulate to dangerous levels in the closed system of the aquarium. This can be prevented by regularly replacing part of the water with fresh. The new water must itself be unpolluted, and of the same chemistry and temperature as that in the aquarium, to avoid stressing the occupants.

Unfortunately tap water may itself be high in nitrates, and, if so, must be treated before use. A variety of equipment is available for this, as well as test kits for ammonia, nitrite, and nitrate, so that the aquarist can monitor water quality.

A new aquarium will not have a population of the bacteria that operate the nitrogen cycle, and must be allowed to mature for 2-3 weeks before it is ready for its occupants. As the cycle establishes there will be toxic peaks in first the ammonia, and then the nitrite, level as the relevant bacteria establish themselves; if fishes are present at this stage they are likely to die of what is termed "New Tank Syndrome". Once nitrite has peaked and returned to safe levels, the aquarium is safe to use.

Internal filter

Internal filter.

mechanical and biological basis. Water is drawn through the filter and any solids it carries are trapped by the filter media, materials designed for this purpose as well as to provide surface area for bacteria to colonise. A filter, like an aquarium, takes 2-3 weeks to become biologically mature (it is usual to mature the two together). Thereafter it is essential to avoid eradicating the bacteria during filter maintenance – no more than half the media should be cleaned or replaced at one time.

Filtration can also operate chemically, for example when peat or limestone chips are used as a

FILTRATION

Aquarists tend to keep more fishes than would be found in a comparable volume of water in nature, and filtration is used to counteract this by optimising the nitrogen cycle, providing the bacteria with additional living space to colonise and a constant flow of oxygenated water (oxygen is necessary to the process). It also carries their "food supply" to them, tidying up the aquarium in the process.

Most filters operate on a

Powerhead for undergravel filter.

Undergravel filter.

filter medium to alter the pH; chemical media will also support mechanical and biological filtration.

A number of different types of filter are available. Power filters may be external or internal, and consist of a canister to contain the media, and a motorised pump to create water flow. A range of sizes is available, and a whole host of media. Undergravel (UG) filters consist of a plate beneath the aquarium substrate, with an uplift pipe through which water is drawn by a rising column of air bubbles or a powered unit ("powerhead"), the substrate acting as the filter medium.

Reverse flow UG pumps water down the uplifts and up through the substrate. Sponge filters consist of a perforated plastic tube fitted with a sponge cartridge; air is pumped through the tube and draws water through the sponge. Box filters (internal and external) are plastic boxes filled with media, and again air-powered. Trickle filters consist of one or more containers of media over which water trickles while exposed to the atmosphere, and may be sited above or below the aquarium. They use a combination of gravity feed and a pump (or power filter) to achieve the necessary circulation.

Nowadays many aquarists make the mistake of assuming that the largest and most powerful filter must be the best for every job. This is not the case. The size and turnover rate of the filter should be matched to the size of the aquarium and the number and type of its occupants, in other words, the mechanical trapping capacity and bacterial population (type and volume of media) together with the oxygen supply (flow rate) should relate to the workload (amount of wastes). Thirty years ago most aquaria were filtered by box filters – if they had a filter at all – yet people nevertheless managed to keep and breed fishes without undue difficulty.

Equally, simple filter media such as foam, floss, or even gravel are adequate for most purposes. No doubt the more esoteric media are as efficient as they claim, but there is no point in spending a small fortune on a degree of efficiency you do not actually need because your fishes are not producing that volume of wastes.

WATER MOVEMENT AND OXYGEN CONTENT

Free oxygen finds its way into water via a number of routes, for example it is produced by plants (during the daylight hours), and absorbed from the atmosphere. The latter method is greatly increased if the water's surface is turbulent, as in a fast-flowing torrent or storm-tossed lake. Slow-moving streams or still pools, by contrast, are likely to have a lower oxygen content. And the higher the temperature of a body of water, the lower its relative oxygen content.

Fishes adapted to high concentrations of oxygen require good aeration in captivity, or they may die; on the other hand, fishes which have evolved to swim peacefully in still waters may experience considerable discomfort if subjected to turbulence. It may be possible to achieve a happy medium, but it is unwise to mix fishes from the two extremes of water movement.

Oxygenation can be enhanced by using the filter return, or an airpump and diffuser, to create movement of the water's surface.

Nowadays most aquarists create far more turbulence than is necessary or desirable for most aquarium fishes. Indeed, it has been found that the long-term stress involved could well be harmful.

TEMPERATURE

There is considerable variation in the temperature of tropical waters, depending on the geographical situation of any particular body of water, its topography, and on a seasonal and daily basis. It is not necessary to reproduce this variation in the aquarium; instead select a temperature which is a reasonable average for the occupants. In general this will be somewhere in the 73-80 degrees Fahrenheit (22.5-26.5 Celsius) range for general maintenance, with a small increase to stimulate breeding, if necessary. Fishes may become sluggish if the temperature is lower than their preferred range, so do not try to reduce the electricity bill by lowering the temperature. Equally, too high a temperature may cause respiratory distress by increasing the metabolic rate and hence oxygen requirement, while reducing the oxygen content of the water.

Equipment

Do not make the common mistake of believing that the more you spend on equipment the more likely your chances of success. Fishkeeping has gone hi-tech only in the last 20 or so years – and yet people were managing to keep and breed tropical fishes very successfully long before the equipment revolution. Even today some of the most successful aquarists have fish-houses full of "antique" and home-made equipment – their secret is that they understand the basic principles involved.

If you are not sure how a piece of equipment works, or you do not know what it is supposed to do, then do not be afraid to ask questions or request a demonstration.

THE TANK

First and foremost you will require a tank, which can be anything from a simple, no-trimmings, glass box to what is essentially the same thing set into a splendid wooden cabinet. In the past, tanks were made by setting panes of glass into angle-iron frames using putty, but nowadays all-glass construction is the norm, the glass being glued together with silicon sealant, a by-product of the US space programme.

Bow-fronted tank.

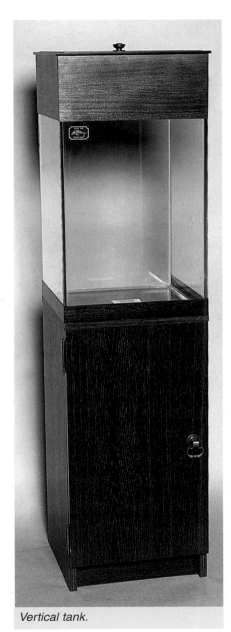

Vertical tank.

You can buy a "brand name" aquarium, but your dealer will probably have a source of locally-made unbranded tanks, often made to order, so you can choose non-standard sizes (but beware, you may not be able to buy a stand or hood to fit). Such tanks are normally cheaper, and generally just as good. Whatever your choice, there are a number of quality checks you should make. Look for scratches – you want new glass, not "recycled" shop windows. Check there are no bubbles in the silicon sealant. All but the very smallest (40 cm) aquaria should have bracing bars along the top of their long sides, and tanks of length (90cm) or more should have a central cross-bar.

Plastic and acrylic aquaria are also available; these are generally small, and, in the case of acrylic, often interestingly-shaped. Although the idea of something more ornamental than a rectangular box may appeal, remember that your primary aim should be to create a home for your fishes, which as an incidental will ornament your home – not to have fishes as incidentals to an ornament! Acrylic and plastic also scratch easily.

It is, however, advisable to purchase a small cheap plastic aquarium to serve as quarantine tank, hospital, and even jail, when required.

THE BASE

You will also require something on which to stand the aquarium (unless it is the cabinet type); it is possible to buy purpose-built welded stands, or you can improvise, provided the base is strong enough to bear the weight involved. Slotted angle iron, wood, even stacks of bricks or breeze blocks can be used if aesthetics are unimportant.

It is essential that the tank itself rests on a flat and even base (otherwise the glass may split), so unless your base already has a solid flat top, you will need a piece of $^5/_8$ in (15 mm) (minimum) exterior grade plywood (other composite boards tend to warp and/or disintegrate if they get damp) at least as large as the tank bottom. Immediately beneath the aquarium you should place a piece of polystyrene foam, again the size of the tank and at least 1/2 in (12 mm) thick, to cushion the glass against any minor unevennesses.

THE HOOD

This is a multi-purpose item which not only keeps fishes and water (by preventing evaporation from escaping) in the tank, as well as dirt, pets, children, etc, out, but also houses the lighting equipment. Hoods are normally made of aluminium and come in standard sizes but varying designs, and it is worth shopping around for one that suits you (in design and/or price) rather than automatically buying the one that may be offered with your aquarium. In particular look for ease of access to your lighting switch and for feeding – you should be able to open the hood with one hand without a poorly-designed knob slipping from your fingers and letting the hood down with a bang to terrify the fishes.

HEATING EQUIPMENT

The commonest method of heating nowadays is with a submersible combination heater/thermostat, but it is also possible to buy an external thermostat and

A heater/stat.

internal immersion heaters, or external under-tank heating mats. None of these systems is perfect. Here are a few of the advantages and disadvantages of each:

Heater/Stats

For: Tamperproof, no electrical connections required.
Against: Heaters have a relatively short life, and you have to buy a new thermostat with every heater. Tricky to adjust temperature.

Thermometer.

External Thermostat

For: Easy to adjust temperature.
Against: Can be adjusted by children and other unauthorised persons. Thermostat may react to room temperature. Has to be connected to separate heaters – wiring skills required.

Under-tank Mat

For: No ugly glass tubes or electricity in the aquarium.
Against: Cannot be replaced without emptying the aquarium!

The total wattage of the heating will depend on the aquarium's size and situation, and should be capable of maintaining the desired temperature on the coldest of winter nights when the central heating is off. Your dealer should be able to advise. If using immersion heating, in all but the smallest aquaria it is preferable to split the wattage between two separate heaters or heater/stats to guard against failure. You will also need a thermometer for monitoring temperature.

LIGHTING

The normal method of illuminating the aquarium is with one or more fluorescent tubes, the size and number being suited to the occupants (fishes and plants). It is essential to use a control unit designed for aquarium use and a potentially damp environment. There is a wide choice of tubes purporting to grow better plants or display fishes in their best colours – at a price. You may prefer to buy a cheap domestic tube from the local hardware store. There is no difference in electrical safety, or, some people would say, in performance! If in doubt, ask to see a selection of tubes in use above the same tank, so you can choose the effect you prefer.

FILTRATION

This is the area of fishkeeping where hi-tech has had the greatest impact, so that today, not only is there a confusing number of different types of filtration available, but each comes in a whole range of products (see Chapter Three).

Far too many hobbyists assume that the biggest most powerful filter is the best for the job, and the profit-motivated trade does little to discourage this view. Twenty-five years ago power filters were a rare luxury and internal air-driven box-filters or primitive undergravel systems the norm, yet aquarists were still able to keep and breed fishes, including some still regarded as difficult today. Some even used no filter at all, relying instead on a skilful balance of fishes, plants, and water changes.

Unless you are planning to start with a very large aquarium or large fishes with messy habits, I suggest that for your first aquarium you use conventional-flow, air-powered UG; you will require UG plates to fit your aquarium, an airpump, and some airline (plastic tubing). UG is very efficient, and the cheapest method to install and run. If you subsequently decide you require something more powerful, or a different type of filter, you can upgrade to powerheads, or remove the uplifts, leaving the plates in place. An airpump is always useful.

You should also buy a non-return valve to prevent water siphoning into the pump in the event of failure or power cut, and, if you require more than one outlet, a set of "gang valves" to split the supply from the pump.

If you want to alter your water chemistry using, for example, peat or limestone chips, then this can be achieved with a simple box filter powered by your airpump. In addition, a box or sponge filter can be kept running in a corner of the aquarium for use in the quarantine/hospital/jail tank when required, avoiding the need for a maturation period before the tank can be used.

BITS AND PIECES

There are innumerable small gadgets available; you may find the following items useful; those marked * are essential:

- Heater holders (to attach the heater/s to the aquarium glass).
- Tube of aquarium-grade silicon

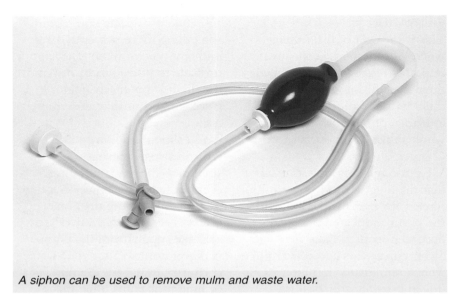

A siphon can be used to remove mulm and waste water.

Equipment for cleaning tank glasses.

sealant (this can be used to stick all sorts of things, e.g. heater holders when the suckers will not grip).
- Algae magnet (to clean the front glass).
- One or more nets of reasonable size (catching a small fast fish in a tiny net is next to impossible).＊
- Valves and clamps (for controlling air flow).＊
- Siphon tube (for water changing).＊
- Plastic bucket (reserved for aquarium use).＊
- Selection of test kits (hardness, pH, and nitrite are essential, nitrate desirable, ammonia optional).＊

Resist the temptation to buy other items until you find you really need them.

You will also need a rubber 4-gang multiple socket with mains lead and plug, for connecting your equipment to the electricity supply. It is possible to buy a "cable tidy" to which everything is wired, but this requires electrical know-how, and causes problems with maintenance – for example, you cannot take a wired-in filter to the sink to clean it out! With a multiple socket you need only be able to wire a plug, and each appliance can be unplugged as necessary.

Do not forget any chemicals or equipment needed to alter the chemistry of your tap water to that suitable for your fishes (see Chapter Three). Finally, some spares are a good idea, such as a heater or heater/stat and a diaphragm for your airpump.

Different-sized nets.

5 *Aquarium Decor*

Y ou will also need some decor to make your tank look attractive, and, more importantly, to help the fishes feel secure and at home. Some aquarists use bare tanks as they believe this makes maintenance easier and improves hygiene. But a bare tank is likely to lead to stressed fishes, and the hygiene idea is a myth. The bacteria which operate the nitrogen cycle are found not only in the filter, but all over the decor, and absence of decor may greatly reduce the biological efficiency of the aquarium. It is true that every vestige of "mulm" (droppings and other detritus) can easily be siphoned off from a bare tank, but remember that fishes also excrete ammonia, and changing all the water daily is not an option!

The psychological benefits of decor cannot be stressed too heavily. In nature there are few creatures that do not have to worry about ending up as dinner for something larger, and this includes most aquarium fishes. They have two main methods of protecting themselves against predation – shoaling, whereby the individual runs a lower risk of predation because of the numbers present, and hiding among natural cover. Some small fishes protect themselves doubly, by shoaling and using cover.

Most, if not all, aquarium fishes are inshore species, which rely on the shelter of the shoreline for safety. Cover may be provided by rocks, plants, dead wood, trailing branches, roots, and holes in the bank. The decor should endeavour to simulate the appropriate cover if possible. Do not worry that your fishes will hide all the time if you provide cover; they may do so at first, finding themselves in new surroundings after a traumatic adventure with a net and polythene bag, but they will soon come out and swim around confidently, because they know they have somewhere safe to go if

necessary. Without decor, many fishes skulk in the back corners, trying to make themselves as inconspicuous as possible.

When planning your decor choose items suited to the fishes, rather than what you think looks nice, though the two need not be totally incompatible. Fishes from a rocky habitat need piles of rocks, while those from densely vegetated biotopes will feel exposed and vulnerable without thick clumps of plants. A mixture of fish types needs a mixture of decor. As long as you provide what the fishes require then there is some leeway as regards personal aesthetics – a rock here and there in a primarily planted tank, or a plant or two in the aquatic rockery, will not distress the inhabitants, even though such items may be alien to them in nature.

Anything you wish to put in the aquarium must be carefully 'vetted' to make sure it will be harmless to the occupants. Materials sold as suitable for aquarium use should be safe – but you must be careful if buying from other sources (e.g. rocks and gravel from a garden centre), or collecting your own.

THE SUBSTRATE

This is the layer of material – usually gravel or sand – used to cover the bottom of the tank. There are three main points to consider when choosing a substrate – colour, grain size, and effect on water chemistry. It is also important, especially if you plan to keep fishes that dig or sift the bottom, or spend time resting on it, to avoid sharp-edged materials which may cause injury.

As regards colour, generally speaking the darker the better. A light, reflective substrate, coupled with the glare of the lighting only a foot or so above, is likely to lead to nervous fishes which pale their own colours to camouflage themselves. A dark substrate will have the opposite effect – relaxed fishes showing good colour and standing out against their surroundings. Remember that, although most sand and gravel is light in colour, in streams and pools it is commonly covered with

a darker layer of leaf litter or other detritus. Unfortunately, dark substrate material is difficult to obtain – most shops stock a varicoloured gravel with a yellowish bias, but this in fact does very well for most fishes.

This "standard" aquarium gravel has a grain size of about 1/8 in (2-3 mm), which is again acceptable for many fishes. You may, however, wish to use a finer material (coarse sand) for fishes which sift the bottom for food, passing the substrate through their gills, or for those with small mouths which need to dig as part of their breeding ritual.

A very fine substrate material will clog more easily than a coarser one, especially with undergravel filtration, while a very coarse substrate will trap particles of food in its interstices, where the fishes may be unable to retrieve them – a pollution risk.

Some substrate materials contain calciferous minerals, which will increase the hardness and pH of your aquarium – not what you want if you are attempting to create soft acid water. Even if the material is sold as "hardness-free", there is a possibility that it is not! Test a small sample by adding a little strong acid to it: if it fizzes, then it is not hardness-free. Because strong acids are dangerous, great care must be taken in making this test, and you may have problems obtaining a suitable acid (any of the major acids such as sulphuric or hydrochloric will do). A good idea is to enlist the aid of your local pharmacist or school chemistry department, who may be persuaded to test a sample for you.

The thickness of the substrate layer depends on whether you are using UG filtration, growing plants, or not. The optimum for a UG filter bed is a thickness of 2.5-3.0 ins (6 to 7 cms). Plants need at least 1.5 ins (3.5 cms) to develop a good root structure, and more will do no harm. But if your main decor is a few rocks and plastic plants, then a token 1 inch (2.5 cms) will be enough.

Finally, a warning about coral sand. Originally sold for marine aquaria, for which it is ideally suited, this material has gained popularity as a substrate for freshwater fishes requiring high hardness and pH. It is, however, very light in colour and reflective, and also lightweight, tiny particles tending to fly up and become suspended in the water, causing skin and gill irritation. If coral sand is required to buffer the water, then 10-25 per cent mixed with an ordinary gravel substrate is adequate, and will avoid these problems. Coral sand should not be used except for tanks where a high hardness/pH is required.

BACKGROUNDS

Your background may be thought of as the bank of your miniature stream or pool, the backdrop for your other decor and, of course, the fishes. It will give your aquarium a sense of direction, the front being the open water into which the fishes venture to feed, the rear their retreat if frightened. Without a background the fishes may be confused as to which way to turn, and hence nervous. "Double-fronted" aquaria, used as free-standing room dividers or set into a wall, are not a good idea from the fishes' point of view.

The background should be reasonably dark (most rocks and soils are!) and natural in colour. It may be a simple external two-dimensional covering for the rear glass, or a complex "sculpted" internal structure. Do remember, however, that anything placed in the aquarium must be non-toxic, and this applies to anything used to colour or waterproof an internal background.

The simplest external background is a coat of paint, though this has the disadvantage that it is difficult to remove if you want a change, or if you wish to turn the tank round at a later date because the original front has become scratched.

Various coverings can be stuck on with glue or tape – e.g. cartridge paper, cork tiles, carpet tiles, or special pictorial backgrounds which can be bought by the foot from most aquatic dealers. Obviously one suited to the rest of the decor will look best.

Examples of internal backgrounds are slates (wedged or glued in place), sculpted and painted styrofoam, or fibreglass mouldings.

Internal backgrounds have the additional advantage that if you take photographs of your fishes you will not be troubled with flash reflections from the rear glass.

THE MAIN DECOR

The main decor falls into two categories: "hard" items, such as rocks and bogwood, and "soft" items, i.e. plants.

ROCKS

In selecting rocks you must again ensure that there will be no unwanted effects on water chemistry. Although few rocks have any significant acidifying effect, some –

You can collect your own rocks.

chiefly limestones of various types – will increase hardness and pH. Rocks such as granite, gneiss, slate, millstone grit, and schists are normally inert. Sandstones may or may not affect water chemistry. If in doubt, put a piece in a bucket of water of known hardness and pH, and check for any increase after a few weeks, or apply the "acid test".

Again, colour is important, though after a while rocks will normally develop a coating of algae on surfaces exposed to the light, and assume a pleasant green – just as in nature. Avoid sharp

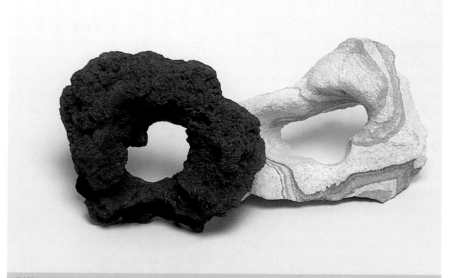

Different shapes create interesting features.

edges which might cause injury, especially if dealing with nervous, lively, or boisterous fishes. Water-worn rocks provide the most natural effect.

Rocks can be purchased in aquarium shops, but are expensive. It is perfectly acceptable to collect your own, provided you have a basic knowledge of different rock types. A small rock identification guide will probably pay for itself in savings on shop costs, with an interesting day out thrown in. Alternatively, a guide to the geology of your area may prove helpful.

Avoid collecting rocks in areas where minerals have been mined – there may be toxic minerals in the bedrock – and beware of veins of crystals, especially coloured ones, though plain white quartz veins are harmless. A quarry is an ideal collecting site. You should be able to enquire what the rock is, and collect loose pieces from an already disturbed environment. Remember that a moss-covered rock lying on the ground is probably home to numerous small creatures, and is best left where it is. Water-worn rocks can be found in rivers (but again may be someone's home), or on the seashore.

SHELLS

Shells are generally not recommended for the freshwater aquarium, as they are composed of calcium carbonate, and will inevitably affect water chemistry. Seashells may also contain salt residues. A few species of fishes, however, utilise shells in nature as shelter and breeding sites, and should be provided with suitable shells in captivity. The empty shells of apple snails, or French edible snails (escargots), are commonly used. They should be sterilised in boiling water before use.

WOOD

Wood, being organic in nature, must be used with care to avoid contamination. Bogwood is sold for aquarium use, but requires considerable preparation before use; although it is semi-petrified, it may still leach tannins into the aquarium, and cause an increase in acidity. Even where this is desirable it is possible to have too much of a good thing, especially on a hit-and-miss basis. So bogwood should be exposed to the elements, or soaked in a bucket of water, for a long period (months rather than weeks), before use. This will have the additional advantage of waterlogging it, so it does not float around the aquarium! Any soft areas must then be carefully scooped out, leaving only hard wood.

Varnishing bogwood is often suggested as an alternative to weathering, but it is difficult to guarantee total sealing because of cracks. And varnish, even if non-toxic in water, may poison any fishes that nibble the wood. Nowadays there are some very good imitation woods available, and you may prefer to use these.

Cork bark is sometimes used as aquarium decor, and should be weathered, as for bogwood. The same applies to driftwood from

Natural wood.

Pipes make good tank ornaments.

the seashore, which, although it has usually been well-weathered already, may contain salt residues. Collect only solid hardwood pieces – pine may still contain resins, which are toxic.

ARTIFICIAL DECOR

Clay flowerpots and pipes make useful caves, and many fishes seem to prefer them to rock structures. They soon become coated with algae and lose their discordant orange look – or they can be concealed under rocks and wood. Use only new ones, to avoid any risk of contamination with pesticides. Clay items sometimes raise the pH, and should be

suspected if this is a problem. Do not use plastic pots and pipes – unless intended for food or aquarium use, most plastics are toxic.

There is also a whole range of

Artificial plants may look reasonably realistic, but they lack the beneficial effects of live plants.

plastic mermaids (for fresh water?!), shipwrecked galleons (ditto), divers, skulls, and other gizmos, many of them designed to emit bubbles if connected to an airpump. These can hardly be described as natural, or beneficial, and are of questionable visual impact – but they do not generally seem to bother the fishes.

Plastic plants are acceptable, but remember that fishes are used to plants being green(ish), occasionally with red markings; not purple, pink, or blue.

PLANTS

Growing aquarium plants can be a hobby in itself, and worthy of an entire book to itself; only the basics can be covered here.

Unless you want to create the

Vallisneria.

Amazon sword (Echuiodorus sp).

perfect simulation biotope for your fishes, you do not need to use plants from their natural waters. As long as there are plants of some kind, greenery-loving species will be confident and outgoing. You must, however, exercise some discretion in your choice of plants.

Firstly, ensure that those you choose are true aquatic plants – some of those sold for aquarium use are not, and soon die if permanently submerged. One or two are actually poisonous! Some of those which are suitable are: *Vallisneria*, *Sagittaria*, *Cryptocoryne*, *Aponogeton*, swordplants (*Echinodorus*), *Hygrophila*, Indian fern (*Ceratopteris*), Java fern (*Microsorium*), *Cabomba*, *Myriophyllum*, *Elodea*, *Rotala* (water wisteria), dwarf lilies (*Nymphaea*), and water lettuce (*Pistia*).

It is normal to plant tall plants at the rear, and sometimes the ends, of the aquarium, shorter ones at the front. But circumstances may dictate alternative arrangements. Plants require a reasonable amount of light for healthy growth, but some fishes do not like bright lights. In this situation, use tall plants whose leaves float on or along the surface, leaving open, shaded, swimming space underneath. Or floating plants such as Indian fern, *Riccia,* and water lettuce.

In order to get the best from plants, research them as carefully as you would your fishes. Some require a large amount of space in order to achieve their potential,

Microsorium pteropus (Java Fern)

others are better planted close together, yet others throw runners and form natural clumps. Light and water requirements vary. Grown properly, plants are an asset, but nothing looks worse than an aquarium with the odd spindly plant here and there.

Until the aquarium is up-and-running you can, of course, only plan your planting – there is no point in buying plants until you have an aquarium in which to put them, as they will not survive long in a bucket in a corner somewhere.

Hygrophila diformis (water wisteria).

6 Setting Up The Aquarium

Setting up a new aquarium requires quite a lot of time, and room to manoeuvre, and it is a good idea to set aside a day for the exercise, and to persuade unwanted helpers such as children and pets to make themselves scarce for the duration. Move as much furniture as possible away from the "site", and ensure you have a clear passage for carrying the aquarium in. Unless it is a small one (30 ins/75 cms or less), you will need a helper to carry and position it.

Make sure everything you need is to hand; not only the aquarium, equipment, and decor, but any tools and bits and pieces you may need, for example, spirit level, electrical screwdriver, scissors, insulation tape, double-sided adhesive tape, electric plugs, cable clips, etc.

It may also be helpful to have a design for your decor in mind – or on paper – though you may prefer to design as you go along. You will not, however, require live plants until the aquarium has warmed up – cold water will do them no good, even if it does not kill them outright. The fishes will come quite a while later, when the tank is mature.

LEVELLING THE BASE
It is important to ensure that the base is level, otherwise the water's surface will be out of true with the aquarium and look very strange, and, in the worst case, the aquarium might topple.

Position the stand or cabinet and check the end-to-end and front-to-back levels with a spirit level. If there is any major discrepancy, then use packing pieces – of solid material and large enough to provide stability – to adjust the feet of the stand/cabinet. If, however, the base is only slightly out of true, then small packing pieces (e.g. coins or metal washers) can be inserted singly between it and the baseboard. Next, set the latter in place, followed by the layer of styrofoam needed to cushion the tank bottom. You may find it helpful to use double-sided adhesive tape to keep the styrofoam in place while you position the aquarium. If using an under-tank heating mat, lay this on top of the styrofoam.

POSITIONING THE AQUARIUM

The aquarium should have no sharp edges, but it is nevertheless sensible to wear stout gloves when carrying and positioning it. You should also wear trousers, long sleeves, and stout shoes, even in shorts and T-shirt weather, just in case of breakages. Glass is dangerous stuff.

Always lift and carry an aquarium by placing your hands underneath it, never by the bracing bars across and around the top – they are likely to break under the weight. Never put an the aquarium down on the ground or floor, however briefly – a piece of grit may damage and weaken

Positioning and levelling the stand.

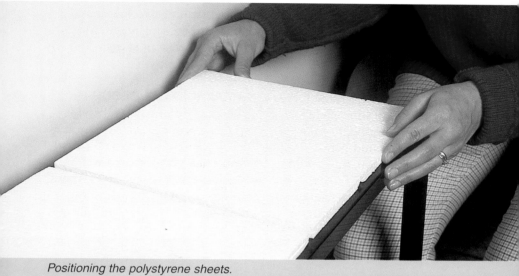

Positioning the polystyrene sheets.

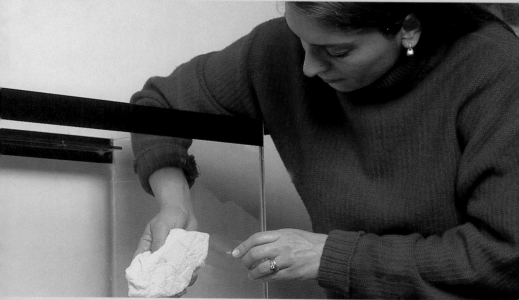

Cleaning the glass.

the glass, with disastrous results later. If you need to put it down, have two smooth, clean, wooden battens, at least as long as the width of the tank and 2 ins x 1in (5 cms x 2.5 cms) or thicker, ready as a temporary resting-place.

It may be appropriate to fit an external background before positioning the aquarium, while access is easy.

Carefully position the aquarium on the styrofoam, making sure that aquarium, styrofoam, and baseboard are all aligned. Make a final check that all is level, and any fine adjustments.

PREPARING THE DECOR
This can be done beforehand if you have somewhere to store the decor where it will remain clean. Wood must be prepared well in advance (see Chapter Five), rocks, flowerpots, pipes, etc must be thoroughly scrubbed, and the

Positioning the tank.

Washing gravel.

for stability and to prevent undermining (by the fishes). You may wish to create a split-level substrate effect by using rocks to create terraces, and this rockwork should be installed at this stage. Do not try to create large differences in levels, though, as over time the substrate tends to level itself out, leaving you with an odd-looking wall which no longer retains anything. Remember to leave room for the plants and internal equipment.

Now add the rest of the substrate, again creating a flattish surface, and any lightweight decor items – small flowerpots, plastic plants, bogwood and cork bark, all of which should be eased into the top layer of substrate. Wood which has not been pre-soaked will float and may need to be wedged in place, or anchored to a

substrate material must be washed. This can be done in a colander under the tap, or in a bucket. It is easiest to wash a small amount at a time, and, if using a bucket, stir vigorously with a plastic spatula or wooden spoon. Keep washing till the water runs clear. The job is best performed outdoors to avoid blocking wastepipes with the inevitable spillages.

INSTALLING THE DECOR

If you have not already fitted your background, do so next. If you are using UG filtration, assemble the plates and uplifts, and position them in the aquarium. You can now add half your substrate material, spreading it evenly over the bottom/plates.

Next, position any large rocks, as well as large heavy pipes and flowerpots, which should be bedded well down to the bottom

Cutting the background to size.

Fixing the background in place.

Putting in the gravel.

stone buried in the gravel, using nylon fishing line.

THE ELECTRICAL EQUIPMENT

The combination of electricity and water can be lethal, so unless you are quite sure what you are doing, you should seek professional advice regarding the electrical connections. If you are using integral heater/thermostat units and a 4-gang socket as suggested, you will need only to know how to wire a plug and fit a fluorescent tube. Separate heaters and thermostats will need to be connected, however. If you do need professional help, ask to be shown how it is done, because you may need to install a new heater "out of hours" at a later date. All electrical connections, plugs, sockets, and non-submersible equipment must be kept out of the water and, as far as possible, out of range of spillages.

Heaters and heater/stats are normally fixed to the back or end glasses using special heater holders. Heater/stats should be positioned horizontally or at an angle, but not vertically, as heat rises and will cause the thermostat to switch off prematurely. Site them as near the bottom as possible, but not contacting the decor, substrate, or glass. If you are using a separate external thermostat, then fit this according to the manufacturer's instructions – there are a number of different types.

You can also position any other internal equipment at this stage: internal filters (duly filled with media, if necessary), airlines (e.g. to UG uplifts), and thermometers. Leads and tubes should exit via the rear corners; the hood, when fitted, will usually have a small gap here to accommodate them. The pipework for external filters – which are normally installed after the aquarium has been filled – can also be fed through these gaps.

Next assemble the hood and

Smoothing out the gravel.

Positioning rocks.

Fixing the heater in place.

Putting the filter in the tank.

The thermometer is fixed inside the tank.

lighting equipment. The hood should be equipped with terry clips to hold a fluorescent tube; if you want multiple tubes then you may have to modify the hood, again seeking professional advice if necessary. The rear part of the hood usually has a compartment for the lighting controller, with holes or slots through which the leads to the tube can be passed. This compartment can also be used to house your multiple socket and airpump, if you so choose. On the other hand, housing electrical equipment in the hood may cause overheating, and involves undue proximity of non-submersible electrical equipment and water, so it is safer to fix these items to the wall behind.

FILLING UP

When filling the aquarium, avoid disturbing your carefully arranged decor by pouring the water over your hand or on to a plate laid on the substrate. Remember to treat

Fitting the fluorescent control unit.

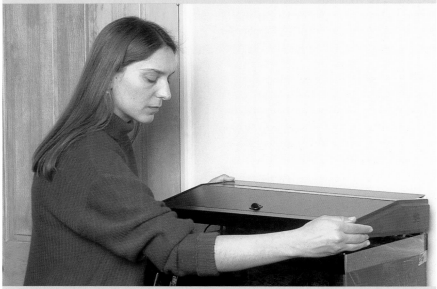

Positioning the hood.

the water beforehand if necessary, though chlorine (but not chloramine) will dissipate long before fishes are added, and you can allow the aquarium to warm up to temperature from cold. Do not, however, adjust water chemistry, as if you buy fishes locally they will almost certainly be in local tap water. You can adjust the chemistry to optimum later.

SWITCHING ON

When the aquarium is filled, complete the installation of equipment. Locate the inlet pipe for any external filter and prime the pump by sucking hard on the outlet pipe to siphon water into the canister (you will have to top up the aquarium afterwards). Connect the airpump, non-return valve, control valves, and air outlets (in that order). Put the hood in place, plug everything in, cross your fingers, and turn the electric supply on. You may need to make some minor adjustments, but air should start flowing, power filters running, and the thermostat indicator light(s) come on. If not, check the following: canister filters sometimes need to be shaken or tipped gently to expel any residual air; the light

controller may need to be switched on; the thermostat turned up if the water is already warmer than its pre-setting. If the heaters are working, you should be able to see warmed water rising from them.

Finally tidy up any excess cabling and airline, "skeining" significant lengths, tying them with adhesive tape or cable ties, and concealing them behind the tank, in the rear hood compartment, or the cabinet. The mains cable, which should have been cut to the required length, should be fixed to the skirting board or floor edge with cable clips.

PLANTING

Once the aquarium has warmed up to running temperature, you can buy and add your plants. Avoid those that have been kept in trays of cold water in the shop – chilling will have done them no good. Instead look for potted plants or those actually rooted in the shop's aquaria; those floating in a warm aquarium are next best.

Before planting, remove potted plants from their pots, and carefully tease away the rooting medium. They will grow much better with their roots free, and

Putting in the water.

MATURING THE AQUARIUM

It takes 2-3 weeks for an aquarium to mature biologically (see Chapter Three), and until it does so, it is not safe to add fishes. This gives you an early opportunity to learn one of the chief skills of fishkeeping – patience!

You will need to give the bacteria something to work on, so add a small pinch of flake food to the aquarium every day. To start with it will lie on the bottom, and may even go mouldy; but, after a while it will disappear – a good sign. Do not rely on hit-and-miss observation though; you should monitor the nitrite level in the aquarium every day. You will find that after a few days of minimal readings it will start to rise; it will usually peak at lethal levels between 11 and 16 days, then revert to minimal. And now, at last, the aquarium is ready for the fishes.

AT LAST, THE FISHES

There is some debate as to whether fishes should be added all at once to a new aquarium, or in small batches to avoid overloading the system. In practice, if the aquarium has been fully matured, and you feed them lightly for the first week or so, the system will

you may find that the pot contains several plants, each of which will do better if given growing space. Those with stems, which are generally sold as (sometimes rooted) cuttings (e.g. *Cabomba*, *Hygrophila*), can simply be inserted into the substrate, but those whose leaves rise directly from the roots (e.g. *Vallisneria*, *Cryptocoryne*, Amazon swordplants) should be planted with their "crown" slightly above the substrate, or they will die.

Planting the tank.

you think sub-standard. Equally, if you want a particular fish, do not be afraid to say so. A good dealer will automatically pick you out both sexes if it is possible to tell the difference, but it does no harm to ask him to do so. Do not be afraid to ask questions; better to display your ignorance than risk the fishes' well-being.

The fishes will be packed in polythene bags and usually brown paper bags or a carrier as well, to reduce stress. Ask for double bags (in case one leaks) and have them "cornered" – the corners tied or taped off to prevent fishes becoming trapped and injured/killed.

If it is very cold or hot, or you have any distance to travel, ask for a styrofoam (insulated) box, or, better still, get one on an earlier visit, and take it with you. Take your purchases straight home, undo the bags, and suspend them in the aquarium for a couple of minutes to let the temperatures equalize. If you have a lot of bags, you may need to siphon off a little aquarium water first, to make room for the water in the bags.

Release the fishes – by submerging the neck of the bag and gently tipping them out – as soon as possible, to minimise

take up the strain without problem. This avoids the need to quarantine new arrivals (to avoid any risk of introducing disease to established healthy fishes); on the other hand, you may want to leave some spare space for any fish that catches your eye later (provided it is suitable for your set-up), in which case quarantine will then be necessary.

When buying fishes, ask to see each one "in the net" (held against the front glass) before it is bagged, and do not be afraid to reject any

Allow the temperature to equalise before releasing the fishes.

The newly-released fishes should be left to settle.

stress. Do not hold the bags up to have a look; do not mix aquarium water with that in the bags over a longer period "to avoid chemical shock" – this will not work unless you take 24-72 hours over it, by which time the fishes will probably be dead of fright. The only way to avoid chemical shock is to make sure the water chemistry of your tank approximates to what the fishes are used to; later on, if you have adjusted your aquarium to optimum for its occupants, then set up your quarantine tank to suit new arrivals, and acclimatize them gradually during quarantine.

The fishes will probably disappear into the decor, and the best thing to do is to put the tank (but not the room) light out, and leave them to it till the next day, when they will have started to settle and can be offered their first small meal. Patience again!

7 *Aquarium Maintenance*

Once your tank is up and running, you must begin a programme of regular maintenance to keep it healthy and looking reasonably neat and tidy. Do not, however, worry about the odd dead leaf or bit of mulm: if you go rummaging about in the tank every day you will disturb – and stress – the occupants. Daily feeding and a weekly maintenance session should suffice.

FEEDING

Feeding your fishes can become one of the great pleasures of your day: they will soon come to realise that you are their benefactor in this respect, and some may learn to feed from your hand. But do not overdo it! Most aquarists overfeed their fishes, and this can shorten their lives, either through causing intestinal upsets, or through fatty degeneration. A wild

Once your tank is ready, do not stress the fishes by too much interference.

Granular food.

fish rarely has the opportunity to overeat. It has to work hard to find enough food just to keep it going, and gets considerable exercise in the process. Look at a photo of a wild fish, or a newly-imported one in a dealer's tank, and you will find its ventral profile, between the pelvic and anal fins, is flat or even slightly

Tablet food.

concave, not well-rounded! That flat profile is the one to aim for, though remember that female fishes may become rounder when full of eggs or fry.

There is now a vast array of prepared foods available for tropical fishes – multiple brands of flakes, granules, pellets of differing shapes and sizes (dried foods); freeze-dried "wrigglies" such as *Tubifex*, brine shrimp, and *Daphnia*; frozen versions of the same. You will also sometimes be able to buy live *Tubifex* (but resist, as these worms often carry disease), *Daphnia*, and brine shrimp.

There is no denying that given the choice, fishes prefer live foods. Even nominally vegetarian species are usually unable to resist food that wriggles, and the psychological benefits are probably as great as the nutritional. To those already mentioned can be added whiteworms (which you culture), earthworms (whole or chopped to mouth size), even spiders, woodlice, and crickets.

Dried foods are normally excellent nutritionally, but can cause constipation and other digestive disorders if fed to excess. A fish may gorge itself on dried foods which then swell in its gut,

Flake food.

so feed only a little at a time.

Frozen foods are generally enjoyed, but have a high water content and are expensive. Nevertheless they can be invaluable for "picky" species when live food is out of season.

To these can be

added a number of domestic foods. Chopped prawn and shrimp are excellent foods, as is mussel. Cod roe is highly nutritious, and a good food for small fishes. Heart, liver, and other lean meats can be fed in moderation, but can cause fat deposits to be laid down if used to excess. Few fishes get to sample cow, sheep, or chicken in the wild!

Vegetarian fishes will enjoy fresh foods such as blanched lettuce and spinach, cooked peas, and slices of raw cucumber and courgette, while piscivores can be given raw cod or coley, whitebait, and the like. Always remember that specialised feeders such as these should be fed primarily a suitable diet, as their digestive systems are adapted to particular types of food.

In general, it is sufficient to feed a small amount once or twice daily, and a quantity that the fishes can consume in 4-5 minutes. You will learn by trial and error – if any food remains uneaten then siphon it off immediately before it pollutes the tank, and watch those fishy waistlines.

Some fishes are nocturnal feeders, so, to avoid their going

Conical worm feeder.

hungry, you may need to give an additional feed (of suitable size) after lights out.

DAILY CHECKS

Learn to regard feeding time as an opportunity to observe your fishes and check that all is well. Make sure they are all present, and check for any signs of malaise that might indicate an incipient problem, such as clamped fins or an increased respiratory rate. There is no need to monitor your water quality daily unless the fishes seem out of sorts, but do check that the temperature is within the desired range, twice daily at lights on and off, and it does no harm to glance at the thermometer whenever you pass the tank.

LIGHTING

In the tropics day and night are of

Siphoning off water

approximately equal length, so your plants and fishes will require about 12 hours of illumination per day, ideally in one continuous period. This does not need to coincide with our daytime, and there is no reason why the aquarium light should not be on when you are there to enjoy it. Avoid plunging the fishes into sudden light or darkness, however, by allowing a five minute dawn/dusk period between switching the room light on or off and the tank light ditto.

MAINTAINING WATER QUALITY

Your filtration system should, if chosen to suit the aquarium, ensure that ammonia and nitrite levels remain minimal – if high ammonia and nitrite are a regular problem, then first make sure that you are not leaving uneaten food lying on the bottom, and if that is not the cause, consider upgrading the filtration. Nitrates, on the other hand, will start to accumulate as soon as the nitrogen cycle is established, and continuing action on your part will be needed to keep them at healthy levels. Aim for a maximum of 25ppm, but the lower the better. Apropos of which, if your nitrate test kit tells

you that you have no nitrate, then replace it. Zero nitrate is impossible in a functioning system, and nitrate test kits seem to have a shorter shelf life than others.

Although there are various gadgets and chemicals available for removing nitrate, the method of choice is simply to change a portion of the aquarium water – usually 10-25 per cent – each week. This not only removes nitrate, but also replenishes trace elements and refreshes the aquarium, rather like letting fresh air into a stuffy room. For this reason it is better to remove nitrates from your tap water, if necessary, and perform a water change on the aquarium, than to simply remove nitrates from the aquarium water. Although your aquarium probably will not need a water change for the first couple of months it is set up, it is better to get into a regular routine and prevent any build-up occurring.

Siphon off the appropriate amount of water, taking the opportunity to siphon off any mulm from the bottom, then refill with clean water of approximately the same chemistry and temperature. Never use water from the (copper) hot water cylinder; it is, however, OK to use a through-flow water heater. Alternatively, you can use water from the kettle to bring cold up to temperature (before adding any to the aquarium), or warm what is required overnight using a spare heater/stat. Remember to eliminate chlorine, chloramine, and other undesirables, if necessary.

When adding new water, siphon it into the aquarium from a bucket standing on the hood, or pour it over your hand, to avoid disturbing the decor and fishes.

FILTER MAINTENANCE

The less often you interfere with your filter the better, as every time you do so you will lose a large number of your filter bacteria, and risk ammonia/nitrite problems while the system recovers. Never clean your filter out completely, or you will have to mature it, and your tank, from scratch, while your fishes experience a nasty case of "New Tank Syndrome". With canister, box, and trickle filters, clean or replace no more than half (one third is better) of the media at a time; gently squeeze sponge filters once or twice in a bucket of aquarium water, and if you have UG filters then do not disturb the

substrate unless it is absolutely necessary. The practice of "hoovering" the substrate with a gravel cleaner every week should be avoided at all costs if you have UG, as this disturbance will prevent the filter from ever achieving any degree of efficiency.

It is, however, in order to replace the contents of chemical filters (those used to alter water chemistry) in their entirety, provided they are not the only form of filtration in the aquarium.

Reduce the loading on your filter following maintenance by reducing feeding for a day or two beforehand, and 2-3 days afterwards, to reduce the fishes' waste output levels.

MAINTAINING THE PLANTS

Aquarium plants will normally thrive on the natural fertiliser produced by the fishes, but if the growth of any plant is meagre – once its roots are established – then you may need to feed it. Avoid fertilisers added to the water, which will cause a nitrate surge; instead use the pelleted type that is pushed into the substrate next to the plant. One or two pellets per plant every 4-8 weeks should be adequate.

You may also need to prune

rampant vegetation and remove dead leaves from time to time.

HOLIDAYS

The danger of overfeeding applies doubly (or more!) to friends and neighbours entrusted with this task while you are away, and, unless you have tiny fry, it is best to leave your fishes unfed if you are away for up to a week. If you do want them fed, measure out daily portions of dried food (small containers or foil parcels) and leave strict instructions that under no circumstances is more than one portion per day to be given. Make these portions about half what you would normally feed. This will avoid any likelihood of accidental pollution during your absence.

Even if the fishes are not being fed, it is a sensible precaution to ask someone to come in once a day to check the temperature and that the filter is running, and to remove any fish that may die (to avoid pollution from the corpse). This person should be competent to deal with any emergency, or have the telephone number of someone who can come and sort out any problem that does occur. If possible, also leave a number where you yourself can be contacted.

An extra partial water change, the day before you leave, will help ensure good water quality until you return; any filter maintenance,

Livebearers are usually easy to breed.

however, is best performed a week or so before your departure so that the filter can return to 100 per cent efficiency before you leave.

BREEDING

If your fishes are properly maintained, then, provided you have male and female, it is probable that at least some of them will breed in your aquarium. Even though most or all of the eggs or fry will perish, usually eaten by their tankmates (or even the parents!), you can congratulate yourself, because the fact that the fishes have bred at all is an indication that the aquarium is to their liking and they are in good health.

A detailed treatise on the breeding of aquarium fishes is, unfortunately, beyond the scope of this book, but suffice it to say that breeding and rearing can add a whole new dimension to an already enjoyable hobby. On the debit side, you will need at least one extra aquarium (the quarantine tank can be used for small-scale operations) with attendant running costs, but the sale of the young fishes will offset these to some degree.

In many instances breeding requires an aquarium, albeit often only temporarily, per species, so you may need to restrict your breeding programme to one or two species initially; if you are a beginner, it makes sense to choose those which are already showing an inclination to spawn. And, as with all aspects of fishkeeping, your chances of success will be greater if you research your subject thoroughly in advance.

Diseases And Other Problems

If your fishes fall ill, then in 95 per cent (or more) of cases the problem is likely to be environmental, that is to say, essentially your fault. If you accept this, then there is a good chance that you may be able to save the affected fish(es), but if you rush to the medicine cabinet and treat with this potion and that, in the forlorn hope of effecting a cure, then you will probably hasten the demise of the unhappy individual(s), and perhaps the rest as well. This is a pity, as a simple partial water change is often enough to solve the problem.

Whenever a fish falls sick, unless it shows clear clinical signs of a specific disease, you should immediately check your ammonia, nitrite, and nitrate levels. If you do have a water quality problem, then stop all feeding, and change 25-30 per cent of the water daily until the readings are acceptable.

In the event of high ammonia and/or nitrite levels, if the problem is a failure of the biological filtration rather than a temporary overload, then twice daily partial water changes may be necessary to save the fishes. If you can borrow a functioning filter, or rehouse the fishes temporarily, then so much the better.

"NEW FISH SYNDROME"

It is all too common for fishes newly introduced to an established aquarium to die within the first few days. Such deaths may be the result of a sudden change in water chemistry or quality, most commonly the latter. The aquarium may have accumulated a high level of nitrates, gradually, so that the occupants have not been seriously affected; the hapless newcomers, however, are used to low nitrate levels, as their quarters have been receiving regular routine water changes plus the replacement of the water used to pack fishes sold. So always check your nitrate levels before buying new fishes, and always ensure that water chemistries are a reasonable match. If not, use your quarantine tank to acclimatize the newcomer(s).

OTHER TYPES OF POISONING

Many domestic chemicals are highly toxic to fishes, for example, paint fumes, furniture polish, household cleaners, insect sprays, etc. If your aquarium becomes contaminated with one of these, then, unless you immediately realise the pollution has occurred, the fishes are probably doomed. Prevention is the keyword. If an accident does occur, then ideally rehouse the fishes while you clean out the tank, or, *in extremis*, do an 80-90 per cent water change (such large water changes should, however, be regarded as a last resort).

As has been stressed earlier, care must also be taken with anything deliberately placed in the aquarium, even the water, to avoid any possibility of poisoning.

PATHOGENIC DISEASES

You may encounter a true fish disease from time to time, although it is often difficult to diagnose exactly which. It cannot be stressed too strongly that there is no point in trying to treat a disease unless you know what it is! Never add a variety of remedies in the hope of effecting a cure – the resulting chemical brew will probably kill fishes which might otherwise have recovered in time.

Do not panic if one fish dies – like us they do not live for ever. But, if faced with an apparent epidemic of a mystery ailment and water quality checks out OK, then consult your vet about the possibility of a post mortem.

The following are a few of the most commonly encountered illnesses.

WHITE SPOT (*ICHTHYOPHTHIRIUS*)

Probably the commonest infectious disease of aquarium fishes. The fish develops pinhead-sized white spots (parasites) which eventually drop off, encyst on the bottom, and after a few days release a host of new parasites. Treatment is by proprietary remedy. If fishes are quarantined, then this disease should never get as far as the community aquarium.

VELVET (*OODINIUM*)

The fish develops a yellowish velvety coating, scratches, and breathes rapidly. Treatment by proprietary remedy; prevention by quarantine.

FIN ROT AND FUNGUS

Although the former is bacterial, these two ailments are commonly seen in conjunction, and are normally indicative of poor water quality, although fungus may affect injuries. Treat by proprietary remedy if the problem is widespread; apply spot treatment with gentian violet in isolated cases. Remedy the cause.

EXOPHTHALMUS OR POP-EYE

One or both eyes protrude from the greatly swollen orbit (socket); the eye(s) may be cloudy. Although this may be caused by an (untreatable) parasite, it is usually a symptom of poor water quality. Recovery may take several days after water quality is improved.

DROPSY

Fluid builds up in the tissues or body cavity, causing swelling,

Trichogaster leeri with tail rot.

Labeo bicolor with dropsy.

particularly of the abdomen. This can be caused by poor water quality, incorrect water chemistry, inappropriate diet, or bacterial infection. The fish sometimes recovers spontaneously if conditions/diet are improved, but usually dies after days/weeks. Euthanasia may be desirable. "Malawi Bloat", which affects some East African cichlids, is similar in symptoms but almost always fatal after 2-4 days. The use of common salt has been identified as an additional cause to those listed above.

SKIN SLIME DISEASE

Tiny parasites (a number of genera are involved, *Costia* being the best known), commonly present in small numbers, multiply and coat the fish, giving it a grey appearance. Normally occurs when environmental conditions are poor. Treat with a proprietary remedy and improve water quality.

FLUKES

These may affect the skin or gills, or both. The fish may scratch itself violently against hard objects; severe cases of gill flukes may cause loss of motor control due to depleted oxygen supply to the brain, resulting from gill damage. Gill flukes are commonly suspected when the problem is actually mechanical or chemical irritation by, respectively, suspended matter in the water or poor water quality/incorrect water chemistry. Flukes can be treated with a proprietary remedy.

SWIM BLADDER DISEASE

The fish has difficulty swimming in the correct position. This may result from injury to or bacterial infection (usually associated with poor water quality) of the swim bladder (the organ of buoyancy), or occur as a side effect of dropsy or digestive problems. Transfer to shallow water with a raised temperature, and/or treatment with a broad spectrum antibiotic, may help, but euthanasia is necessary if there is no improvement within a week.

DIGESTIVE PROBLEMS

The fish becomes sluggish, sometimes shows a slightly distended belly, may rest on the bottom, refuses to feed, and may produce abnormal or no faeces. Caused by incorrect diet or overfeeding. The fish may recover spontaneously, and treatment with half a level teaspoonful of Epsom Salts (Magnesium Sulphate) per gallon (4.5 litres) will do no harm. In the long term, improve the diet and feeding regime.

MEDICINES

Nowadays there are proprietary treatments for most diseases and parasites you are likely to encounter, although some (e.g. antibiotics) must still be obtained from the vet. Not all treatments are suitable for all types of fishes, so always check.

There is no point in keeping an array of treatments "just in case". Most have a shelf life, and if you do not have them, you will not be tempted to use them before you have established what the problem really is. Unless you live in a very remote area, you will probably have a dealer somewhere locally open every day of the week, so you can buy medicines as and when required.

Remember that some diseases tend to affect fishes only when they are stressed by environmental problems, and remedy the cause as well as treating the symptoms.

Always follow the manufacturers instructions regarding dosage, and always complete the full course of treatment. Bear in mind that some medicines may eliminate friendly filter bacteria as well as hostile pathogens; if possible, select one that is safe, or use your quarantine tank as a hospital.

EUTHANASIA

If a fish is badly injured or very ill, or can no longer swim properly, and there is no sign of recovery beginning, then it is kindest to put it out of its misery. It can be humanely despatched by cutting through the spine just behind the head – death is instantaneous and definite. Alternatively ask your vet for assistance.

OTHER PROBLEMS

POWER CUTS

Do not panic! Aquaria can survive several hours with the power off. First establish that the problem is not at your fusebox, then phone the electricity company to notify them of the loss of supply. Tell them you have tropical fishes, and ask them to let you know the likely duration of the power cut – you may have to call back for this information. Insulate the tank with blankets, quilts, sleeping bags etc. If the cut is a long one and the weather cold, use plastic

bottles or polythene bags, filled from the domestic hot water tank and stood/suspended in the aquarium, as heaters.

It is worth obtaining a battery-operated airpump for such emergencies, or you can aerate the tank every half hour or so using a bicycle/car/airbed pump. Your filter bacteria may be affected by the lack of oxygenated flow through the filter, especially if the cut is a long one (more than two hours), so reduce or stop feeding and keep a check on water quality for two to three days.

EQUIPMENT FAILURES

Always keep a spare heater and, if appropriate, air pump diaphragm, at the ready. If a major item fails outside shop hours, then see if your fishkeeping friends can help by lending you a spare or even accommodating your fishes temporarily. And, if you are a good customer of a local dealer, he will probably not mind helping you out even outside business hours.

ALGAE

Algae are primitive plants which will always grow where there is water and light, so unless you plan to keep your fishes without one or both – not a good idea! – then you must learn to accept algae as inevitable. Or better, as a friend. Algae will give your hard decor a natural look; being plants, they will use up some of the nitrates your aquarium is producing – and, if they become too rampant, warn you that you may have too much nitrate present. Some of your fish will nibble at the algae, which will also harbour micro-organisms to help feed any fry that come along. So keep the front glass clear for viewing, and leave the rest alone.

Algae can sometimes cloak plants, apparently retarding their growth. But if the plants were thriving then they would be producing new young leaves as fast as the algae colonised the older, already dying, ones. Often plant growth is poor because the aquarist has reduced the light to prevent algae, when he should have increased it to assist plant growth.

"Blue-green algae", not really algae at all, is, however, a real problem if you are unfortunate enough to be afflicted by it, coating everything with a blanket of slimy blue-green. It is difficult to eliminate, but reducing nitrates to a minimum, and cleaning away as much of the mess as possible on a regular basis (it can be sucked away with the siphon) will usually do the trick – eventually.

AND FINALLY...

Although this final chapter – and indeed this book – may have given the impression that fishkeeping can be full of pitfalls, be reassured that, if you are meticulous and methodical in the setting up and maintenance of your aquarium, you can look forward to a rewarding and enjoyable hobby. The trick is to avoid those pitfalls, and hopefully this book will help you to achieve that goal.